Customer Service Excellence For World-Class Security Officers

Skills & Attributes of a
World-Class Security Officer

by

The Customer Service
Training Institute

All rights Reserved 2013
The Customer Service Training Institute

Other Customer Service Training
Manuals from
The Customer Service Training Institute

Customer Service Basics

Service Recovery Skills

How to Interact with All Kinds of Customers

Enhancing the Customer Experience

Customer Service Training for Managers & Supervisors

Customer Service Training for Service Technicians

Customer Service Training for the Hospitality Sector

Customer Service Training for Health Care Professionals

Customer Service Excellence for Security Officers

Safety in the Workplace

"Security is more than just protection. It also involves making people feel safe and secure in their workplace and wherever they might go"

Table of Contents

Introduction	7
The Importance of Perception	10
Part One Personal Attributes	13
Self Confidence	19
Attitude	21
Professionalism	23
Personality	27
Honesty & Integrity	30
Calm & Controlled Under Pressure	34
Ability to Lead & Take Charge	38
Have Common Sense	41
Physical Fitness	44
Positive Image	49
Appropriate Values	53
Part 2 Skills Needed	55
Experience	57
Training	63
Observation & Comprehension	65
Fast Thinking	69
Taking Initiative	72
Part 3 Conversation Skills	74
Be Good With Names	76

Be Personable yet Professional	79
Greeting People	82
Interacting with Different People	84
Listening Skills	88
Remaining Calm	94
Tact and Reasoning	99
Be Easy to Understand	103
Effective Body Language	107
Confrontation Management	113
Empathy	119
Legal Issues and Considerations	121
Conclusion	123

Disclaimer

This publication is designed and intended to be used as a resource to aid in the development and training of security officers. Not everything in this manual will be applicable and appropriate for all situations, locations, and applications. It is the sole responsibility of the security officer or company to ascertain the proper use and application of any or all of the information within this publication. The writer, printer and distributor accept no responsibility for the results of the application or use of any of the techniques or concepts explained or discussed in this publication.

Introduction

Though this might seem extremely basic for some of you reading this book, before we can determine what we must do to become a World Class security professional, we first must understand what security is both to us and our clients.

Security can take on many different forms. From a person in charge of walking a shopping mall and keeping order to protecting millions of dollars in currency or precious objects. There is a human element as well in most security positions and that is protecting the health and welfare of the people you are given responsibility for.

These responsibilities, no matter how important or even as trivial as they might seem, should ever be taken to for granted. How you view your job, and the tasks that go along with it, will play a huge role in how well you perform.

Though the various activities and responsibilities of any security guard can vary widely, there are a few things that remain the same whether you are responsible for guarding $50 or $500,000,000.

The first thing you need to understand is that security professionals, and their companies, provide more than just security of people, money, and personal property. They also provide safety, peace of mind and reassurance. In many respects those three items are at the core of every security job and every security professional's job. If you are capable of only providing one or two out of the three, chances are you will not go far in this industry.

That might seem to some of you as a very harsh statement. Well, it is harsh because those three items, safety, peace of mind and reassurance are what almost 100% of your clients are demanding from their security professionals.

Think about something for a moment. Place yourself in the position of a client for a moment. Let's say someone wants to have some very expensive and important property protected for some reason. You are assigned to the job and you are very competent in every face of providing this type protection. But something in the way you go about performing your duties makes the client question your abilities or effectiveness. As a result they worry constantly that something will happen and that their property is at risk.

In this case you are providing security but not peace of mind or reassurance. How likely do you think it will be that you will be re-hired in the future, or even continue on this job right now? Depending on the people involved and the situation, they just might go elsewhere for their security needs.

Security is one of those services and industries where how you do things are just as important as the results you produce. A manufacturer could have the worst staff imaginable and the dirtiest factory but if somehow they produce a good product, no one cares. But if you do not project confidence and inspire safety and peace of mind, it might make little difference that you did protect the people or property.

The Importance of Perception

The entire Security Industry is one extremely based and judged on perception. What this means is that it is not enough to do your job well, you must also convince the client that you know what you are doing and that you are extremely competent at what you do.

Security companies get business based on their reputation in their towns and within their industry. Those reputations are built, and also damaged, by those who perform the services for the client. It is also important to understand that reputations can also be built and ruined on perception as well. It is not fair, but it is the reality.

We are telling you this not to scare you or intimidate you, but rather to make you aware that as a security professional, the way you go about performing yourself and conducting yourself has a significant impact on both the quality and perception of the service you perform.

There are a lot of people who feel that as long as they do a good job, nothing else matters. For security professionals, nothing could be farther from the truth. For security professionals, we have to look our best and act our best every single minute we are acting on behalf of a client. We cannot turn on and off our professionalism or conduct.

We need to be at our best at all times because we never will know when someone will see us or interact with us in some way that might cast a negative shadow on the rest of our work.

Take a look at this example:

A Security Guard is entrusted with guarding some valuable paintings stored in a local warehouse. The guard patrols the area in a totally professional manner all day and into the night. He is relieved at 10PM for a one hour lunch break. Instead of eating, he is exhausted so he goes out to his car and takes a nap. He comes back refreshed after 55 minutes and completes the rest of his shift.

Now this guard did nothing wrong. He took his break as scheduled and only when his relief person showed up. But suppose someone walking by snapped a picture of him sleeping in his vehicle? Or even worse, took his or her cell phone out and shot a video and uploaded it to an online video sharing site. All you need is a title like "Security Guard sleeps while $$$$$ of paintings go unguarded" and you have a real issue.

When people see the video or read the story in a local newspaper, it will make no difference to them whether you did anything wrong or not. They will not care that you had back-up taking your place. It will make no difference to them that the paintings were never unguarded. But the perception to anyone seeing the picture or the story will likely be the same. That perception will be that your security company hires people who sleep on the job. It can take a lot of time and effort to reverse that perception.

This manual is going to go over a lot of different things that go into just how our clients and customers feel about the quality of our service. You might feel some are silly, or downright stupid and even baseless. But you know what? What you and I think really doesn't matter! Because we are not the ones who make the decision to hire us or our company. That decision is made by the companies and consumers who hire us so it is what THEY think that is important.

So let's put our egos and feelings aside and take a look at a few things from a client's point of view.

Part One
Personal Attributes

In order to be a good and effective Security Professional, there are certain personal attributes that usually go hand in hand with providing security. These are those things that we are born with and also things that we can learn over time.

Personal attributes help define us as a person. Personal attributes help distinguish us from others and help people form a perception on who we are and how effective we might be in our chosen profession or in anything else in life.

Most of these attributes can be changed and developed to help us create the individual we truly wish to be. We can learn from others and change things that might be viewed as negatives and improve things that are usually seen as positives.

Keep in mind that the way we present ourselves to others plays a powerful role in developing a positive and proper perception about ourselves with others. The more we pay attention to how we act and react in life, the better we will be able to do our jobs and deal with those things that life throws at us.

The following pages list the most important personal attributes when it comes to being a truly world class Security Professional.

Professional Appearance

It has often been said that you only get one chance to make a first impression. With that in mind, let's just say that as a Security Professional, you will have an opportunity to sometimes make hundreds, even thousands, of first impressions every single day.

Like it or not, the way you look has a profound influence in the way people see you. Your appearance should be appropriate for the type of work that you are doing at the time. That includes the way you dress, the way you are groomed and the way you are viewed by others in general.

When we say your dress should be appropriate for the type of work you are performing at that time, we mean that the clothes you wear should be deemed proper and normal for that type of work. For example, if you were an auto mechanic, coverall or jeans would be considered acceptable and normal.

If you were a loan officer at a financial institution, then a suit and tie might be considered normal and appropriate. You wouldn't expect your mechanic to be in a suit and you wouldn't want to invest with someone dressed in greasy jeans and a t-shirt!

As far as Security professionals are concerned, dress and attire will depend greatly on the work you are being assigned to do. If you are a security guard in a store or mall, for example, then you likely would have a uniform that would readily identify you as a guard. This is done so that your presence will be known as both a deterrent and so people will know who you are in case they need help.

But if you are assigned to guard an individual, it might not be desirable for you to wear a uniform as your client might wish for you to blend in and not be readily identified as a security officer. In these cases, your attire would be suitable for the event or situation or whatever the client requests.

Sometimes clients or retail businesses want their security people to blend in so it would be easier to identify and apprehend shoplifters. In these cases, you would dress like the average customer in that type of retail establishment. The entire idea here is for you to blend in and not be noticed. The same would apply to any kind of surveillance activities.

Usually you will be given instructions on how to dress and what your appearance needs to be for your particular assignment or situation.

Listen to and follow those instructions to insure your dress is appropriate for what you will be doing.

It is always important to keep in mind that your personal style is of no concern to your customer or client. You need to dress like THEY want to see you and the way THEY feel inspires confidence. Save your personal dress preferences to your personal time not while you are on the job. This is not an infringement on your personal rights; it is just giving the customer or client what they expect from their security team.

Regardless of what you are wearing, there are a few more items relating to your appearance that should always be a factor. Some of these are:

Personal Grooming

Regardless of what you are doing or how you are dressing, unless some special situation requires otherwise, you should always be neatly groomed. Faces should be freshly shaven and washed, teeth cleaned, hair combed or styled, and the type and length of hair appropriate for the assignment.

3-day beards might be the current style and might be viewed attractive by some but for security purposes, a neat and clean look is important.

Cleanliness

Always shower and be clean for any assignment.

Body odor is a definite turnoff and can project an overall very poor image. Keep hands clean and fingernails neatly trimmed. Wash face and hands as well.

Uniforms or other garments should also be neat and clean. Wrinkled garments should be ironed or pressed. Shoes should be shined if applicable and anything that is worn, dirty, or disheveled should be addressed. This is vital for your overall look and the impression you give out to others.

Professionalism

How you look and act should inspire and project professionalism. Remember that while you are providing security services that making people feel safe and secure is part of your services. In order to accomplish that you not only have to look the part, you have to act that way as well.

Inspiring Confidence

When it comes to your appearance, everything about your appearance should shout out confidence. People should look at you and feel confident in your abilities and that you are capable of keeping them safe and secure. So look at yourself in the mirror and look past your obvious good looks and see what you can do to make your overall appearance better and more professional.

Definite Things to Avoid

Remember that you are projecting professionalism and security. So unless a particular assignment requires it, stay away from T-shirts with messages, slogans and logos on them. Also leave your logo ball cap at home and stick to either your uniform hat or a plain hat. Remove any noticeable piercings and cover up any visible tattoos as well. You would be surprised at how people react to some of these things. (It is not usually a positive reaction!)

Lastly, always adhere to the rules and policies of your company when it comes to personal appearance and dress. These rules are usually the result of long time experience and the wishes and directives from both past and current clients.

Self Confidence

A security professional must always be self-confident in his or her abilities to provide the services and protection expected. Your clients and customers want to feel secure and well protected while you are performing your duties.

Self-confidence should never be confused with arrogance, however. Arrogance is a huge turnoff for most people and it should be avoided at all costs. You can be very self confident without being arrogant.

When someone is confident in their abilities and skills, they are more apt to move forward with conviction and make important decisions with little or no hesitation. Self-confident people do not look for approval or validation for what they do before they do it. They assess a situation, know what to do, and make the required choices almost immediately.

When it comes to security services, confidence provides another very important benefit to your customer or client. Confident people do not panic and are not indecisive.

When people are nervous or perceive they are in danger, they look for people who are strong and confident in their abilities. They look for people who do not panic and who know what to do.

Security professionals are the people who are looked to for guidance and direction when other people around them are afraid or don't know what to do. When you are in one of those situations, if you appear frightened or nervous in your abilities, the people who look to you for help will become more frightened as well. If you remain calm and poised, those around you will likely stay calmer as well.

Lastly, people who are confident and act confident will have a much greater chance of being listened to. If people feel that you know what you are doing they will be more likely to listen to you.

Let's say you are in a situation where there is a danger to those around you. Maybe there is a robbery or a shooting at a store and you need to get people to safety. If you are confident and act in that manner, people will follow your directions and commands a lot more than if you are panicking and nervous.

Your primary responsibility is providing a safe environment for those in your responsibility. Behaving in a reassuring and confident manner is the very best way to getting people to listen and follow your directions.

Attitude

As with almost any other profession or occupation, your attitude is very important to your overall success. When it comes to security professionals, however, attitude takes on a whole new dimension.

When you are responsible for the safety and well being of people there will be times when you will be called upon to take action that involves other people. How you go about this will have a significant effect on how those actions are perceived.

Your attitude will also influence how people react to you and how they feel about you as well. Because of this we should take steps to make sure we project the best overall attitude so that we can be our most effective as a security professional.

Authority

Security professionals are looked upon as authority figures.

Just how much will depend on the level of service and the type of situation but every security person is viewed as an authority figure at some level.

This does not mean that you should place yourself at a higher level than those whom you serve. You should not act like you are better or more important than anyone else or "throw your weight around" because you have some authority. Most people will recognize this type of behavior almost immediately.

In fact, security professionals should place their clients and customers at a higher level and do whatever needed to make sure they provide the highest level of protection and service to them. There is no room for egos in security and there is also no room for people to use their position as someone in authority to hold it over others.

This does not mean, however, that we should adopt and "anything goes" mentality when it comes to our customers and clients. We need to have a relationship where we can let them know when they are doing something that places them in danger or makes them more vulnerable. But when those situations arise those statement should be made with diplomacy and tact.

Professionalism

We should always remember that when we are on the job our primary function is attending to the safety and security to those we are responsible for. Whether it is the people at the local mall or a high level protection detail, we must always act in a professional and confident manner in protecting those in our charge.

That usually means keeping some kind of "distance" emotionally from those we are protecting. Sometimes, especially in long term assignments, this can become a problem as we may develop friendships with the same people we are protecting.

We should always make sure our primary focus is on being a security professional and not a buddy or friend. When we start acting like friends our focus shifts from providing security to being a friend and that most often is not the best situation to be in. We often find ourselves letting our guard down and placing others at risk.

It is perfectly fine to be friendly and pleasant with others as long as the focus stays on the security and well being of others. Making sure that everyone plays by the same rules and no exceptions are made is the best way to insure the safety and security of others.

Confidence

We have already talked about being confident in our abilities. We must be confident in order to do what we do efficiently and to the best of our ability. We need to be able to be decisive and act quickly because we know what to do and how to do it.

If there are things that you are not confident about in your day to day security duties, talk to your supervisor about them. Getting additional training or talking to others to get ideas and guidance is a great way to gain the self-confidence you need.

Confidence comes with experiences and proving to yourself that you are good at what you do. Nothing accomplishes this better than time and experience. As we said before, though, do not let arrogance get in the way of your thinking. Always be honest with yourself and keep an open and honest eye on your abilities.

If you go through a difficult situation where you think you might not have done your best, go back over things and determine what might have been done differently or better. Then the next time you find yourself in a similar situation you can draw from your experience and perform better.

No one knows everything but those who admit that and learn from their mistakes are the people who make the best performers and the best professionals.

Another great way to gaining the confidence you need to is to continually improve your skills and abilities. Take courses and seminars in the latest security technology and techniques. Listen to others and read books to broaden your knowledge and abilities. Never be satisfied and always keep improving. If you do that, confidence will cease to be an issue with you.

Empathy

It is perfectly fine to feel bad for others and to tell them that you feel their pain. As human being we all feel for others when something bad or unfortunate happens. That is just human nature.

But we need to find a way to separate empathy, feeling bad for someone, and sympathy, feeling bad and wanting to do something to help them. We need to do this because sometimes we have rules, regulations, and legal requirements that prevent us from making certain statements or taking certain actions.

For example, if we tell someone that we feel bad and that a certain rule is "stupid" or that we wish we could do a certain thing for them because of their problem, then that could be used in court if a lawsuit was brought against the client.

While that is unfortunate, it never the less is the way the world works today. Many a person has made a well intentioned comment intended to make someone feel better only to have it used against them in a court of law.

The best way to deal with unfortunate situations or when something bad happens to someone else is to show empathy and let them know you feel bad for them but to stop right there. Do not make any other statements or promise or tell them you wish you could do something for them.

I know this might sound cruel and even a bit heartless but remember your primary function is to provide security and assistance and not to take responsibility when things go wrong or provide solutions for customer problems.

Personality

For a security professional, an outgoing and pleasant personality will help you accomplish more and perform at a higher level. Personality is important because the way you act with others will determine how effective you are likely to be in providing a secure and safe environment.

Security professionals need to be able to establish a rapport with the people they interact with. Their personality must be one that allows them to inspire respect and confidence while not intimidating people who need their help or assistance. Keep in mind that your interaction with your clients and customers should be viewed as a positive experience. You should be someone they like to see not someone they ignore or avoid.

Your personality should make people feel comfortable around you while still keeping the boundaries that need to exist between security professional and client intact.

If the people you encounter are long term clients, such as residents of a building that you see every day, being able and willing to greet them by name in the morning would be appreciated and help create a good relationship. Sometimes you will be the first person they see at the start of a long day and seeing a friendly face and hearing a warm greeting just might make them smile.

As previously stated, your personality should inspire confidence but not be too hard or too rigid. While there will be assignments and clients who want a "no nonsense" guard, most assignments will benefit from having someone who puts people at ease.

Part of your personality is the attitude you have regarding yourself and those around you. You should have confidence in yourself without appearing over confident or condescending. People will almost always spot someone who feels they are better than everyone else and that is not good in any career, especially security.

It is also important to understand that some aspects of security benefit from a knowledge of the people you are protecting. Being able to know each person and their habits and mannerisms might help you uncover a potentially serious or abnormal situation. The more you know about the people you are protecting, the more likely it will be that you will spot something that is not right.

There are many different parts of your behavior and thinking that make up your personality. Anything that makes people develop confidence and respect for you is good and should be encouraged. Anything that makes people want to avoid you or become afraid of you should be changed.

Sometimes those people around you are the best judge about how your personality is viewed by others. We tend to not see our own faults and consulting others can provide us with some valuable insight. So ask your family, friends, and even your supervisor or manager for some feedback. Then take action to address any negatives that might exist so you can become a more effective security professional.

Honesty & Integrity

We probably should have made this the first item in this section or possibly the first item in the entire book because honesty and integrity are the most important personal attributes a security professional can possibly have.

When you stop and think about it, security professionals "sell" honesty and integrity. You are there to protect and to help others obey rules and policies. You are there to safeguard money, valuable and other items during transport, storage or exhibition. You may also be entrusted with classified or confidential information. Because of this, you need to be trusted.

We have talked about perception and how important it is to have a positive and proper perception of ourselves and our company. When it comes to honesty and integrity, perception takes on a new and even more important meaning.

Everything we do must showcase our honesty and create a perception that our honesty and integrity is above reproach.

We cannot and should not bend the rules for ourselves or friends or even the people we know. Bending or breaking any rule calls our integrity.

For example, if there is a rule about not smoking in the building and you are seen sitting at the security desk with a cigarette then you give the impression that the rules are not meant for you. Or if you go out the emergency exits and block them open to take a shortcut to get something from your car, which is not good either. This may seem trivial, but if you demonstrate that the rules apply only to others and not yourself, your credibility and integrity come into question.

Having honesty and integrity also means never accepting gifts or bribes for "looking the other way" or allowing people to bend or break rules. Though this may place you in awkward positions at times, you must always remind people that the rules and policies are there for a reason and that you are there to make sure everyone, without exception, follows them.

Security professionals are the ones who must take charge during emergencies and also are called upon to enforce the rules. To be effective at these tasks, you have to be respected and trusted and be thought of as someone who enforced the rules and regulations fairly and across the board without exception.

Security professionals must inspire confidence and be trusted above everything else. There should be no apprehension or concern when it comes to the sharing of confidential information.

Because of the extreme importance attached to honesty and integrity, you must be very aware of what you are doing 100% of the time. Even an innocent mistake, if noticed by the wrong person, can come back to hurt you.

Here are a few suggestions to follow when it comes to protecting your honesty and integrity while on the job.

Know the rules and policies in place where you are working.

Follow every rule to the letter while on and off duty.

Report any issues or infractions promptly regardless of who performs them.

Do not make exceptions for friends or people you know.

If someone wants to break a rule, explain that the rules are there to protect them.

If something doesn't look right, report it or take action to investigate.

Pay attention to what is going on around you. That means no long personal calls or conversations that might distract you.

Report any bribes or gift offers immediately.

Do not accept any gifts without approval of your manager.

Lastly, keep in mind that even innocent things can be turned around and used against you if you are not careful. Even something as innocent as a Christmas gratuity might be turned around by a lawyer to be a payment for doing something you shouldn't. Protect yourself, and your company, by understanding the policy regarding tips and gifts. Report any offer or gift to your supervisor and ask permission to accept it.

Regardless of whether you are allowed to keep the gift or not, never allow those giving you gifts to break or bend the rules because they give you gifts.

Calm & Controlled Under Pressure

The ability to remain calm and controlled under pressure is not a suggested skill or attribute but rather a REQUIRED one! Security professionals are people who are in place because there is a possibility that an incident will take place where assistance and support will be needed. It just makes sense that the people who are called upon to provide those services are able to do so in a calm and confident manner.

When we are placed in tense or dangerous situations, many people tend to get nervous and panic. When the human brain is in that kind of state, rational and normal thought is almost impossible. When we are scared or nervous or frightened, we tend to act on impulse. The technical term for this is a **fight or flight response**. That means we either run away from trouble or confront it head on. Neither might be the appropriate response.

People who remain calm, however, tend to evaluate the situations and rationally think about what they need to do before doing it.

The results are almost always better than an impulsive response.

Take a fire for example. If you get scared and upset your first instinct might be to open the door and run into the hallway. But that could mean letting the fire into your room or at least introducing a new source of oxygen into the fire causing it to explode. Neither option is likely going to be good for you.

But someone who is calm will take the time to feel the door before opening it to see if it is hot meaning there is fire on the other side. They would look for other alternative escape routes. If the door was the only option, they might wrap themselves in wet towels to reduce burns. Regardless of what precautions or thoughts are involved, the results are almost always better when calm people make rational judgments.

Another reason to remain calm and controlled is speed of action. Calm people who know what they are doing and can think in a rational and controlled manner will be able to make decisions faster and more accurately. The result is that more people are brought to safety faster and less people remain in danger.

People who panic tend to hesitate. If you do not know instinctively what to do, hesitation can place people in more danger. When people look to you for help or assistance, being calm will enable you to provide the help faster and with more accuracy.

As a security professional, you will be called upon to provide guidance and assistance for groups of people.

Because the security person is a person of authority, you will be called upon to direct people to do certain things or show them the preferred course of action. Remember you are not only helping yourself but others as well.

Another important reason for remaining calm and controlled while under pressure is that calm people tend to create more calm in others. When you encounter someone who is calm and tells you that everything will be fine if you follow their instructions; that will tend to make you calmer as well.

Calm people are almost always less prone to panic and rioting. The last thing we need when we are in a dangerous or uncontrolled situation is someone screaming and panicking and inciting others to take drastic or unwise action.

Being able to keep calm is the result of two primary factors. The first is that you have faith and confidence in your ability to handle most situations. The second is that you have either the training or the experience that enables you to know what to do in these types of situations. The combination of these two factors lets you feel that you are prepared to handle what you are up against.

The primary reason people panic or get afraid is the unknown. You are likely no different. Once you receive the training, or have experienced something, you will be more prepared to handle the same thing in the future.

If you are someone who panics under pressure, you should ask yourself why.

It doesn't mean you are a bad person or ill equipped to be a great security person, it just means there are issues that need to be explored and addressed.

Usually additional training will be a great help. Familiarizing yourself with emergency response plan and policies will also be a great help. These plans and procedures were developed to help people in times of crisis and danger. They have been created by professionals and tailored for the specific client or building you are working in. Know them like the back of your hand so you can act quickly when needed.

Ability to Lead & Take Charge

Security professionals are the people that others look toward when as crisis arises. Whenever a situation arises that places people or their possessions in danger, they look to security for answers and direction. The health, safety and well being of others will often depend on your ability to seize control of the situation and lead others in the right direction.

As the security professional on site, you need to be the person to step up and take charge. You cannot be the one who stands in the background and lets someone else give direction. You are the first line of defense and the one who must initially provide guidance, instruction and direction.

In some cases you will be called upon to enforce policy, procedures and orders from others.

In these times you will need to take those orders or directives and see that people adhere to them and follow them in an orderly fashion.

This will require leadership skills. You need to be able to inspire people to act the right way and to avoid panic.

Sometimes you will be a part or member of a security team. In these cases you will be expected to perform your specific role within that team and work with others to see that everything is done according to plan and directives. That means working with others and organizing efforts to make sure everything is done properly and nothing is forgotten or omitted. Every group needs a leader, or sometimes multiple leaders, to insure that the group will function at their best during any situation.

The safety and well being of others, as well as the security of possessions and physical goods hinges on how well you are able to make sure everything is handled quickly and properly. You must be able to identify the needed course of action and see that this is followed for the common good.

A great leader sees the whole picture and instinctively knows what needs to be done and how to make sure that the situation is resolved with the safety and well being of all involved. A great leader will understand the strengths and weaknesses of the people in the team and use them to their greatest advantage.

A vital function of a security person is to create and maintain order. That means to see that the situation is stabilized as quickly as possible and that everything is being done and accomplished in an orderly manner.

It also means quieting and calming down people and establishing open lines of communication.

The ability to lead and take charge requires that the person be able to evaluate the particular situation and have the expertise and knowledge required to determine the proper course of action.

This means complete knowledge of any rules, policies, and procedures currently in place and approved by the client or establishment. It also requires good communications skills and the ability to reassess and modify plans according to specific situations.

The ability to become an effective leader also requires self confidence, experience and the ability to act with conviction. This is developed over time by experiencing various situations and learning effective ways to handle crisis.

One important thing to remember when you are trying to lead people is that respect is not demanded, respect is earned. People will rally around you once they determine that you are the right one to lead them to safety or towards their objective. A uniform or badges are just objects. It's the person behind them that matters the most.

Have Common Sense

Very few things in life go exactly as planned. No matter how much we try, how much we research and how careful we are, we can never ensure that anything will always go as planned.

Because of this, rules, procedures and directions must often be modified or even scrapped entirely when a situation calls for it. We cannot rely on a book or a manual to guide us through every variation of every situation.

That's why security professionals need to improvise and be able to think on their feet and react properly. This is a skill that relies heavily on training, experience, confidence and most of all, common sense.

Having common sense means that you have a pretty good idea of the right way to act or react in any given situation. While you might not know exactly what needs to be done, you can rely on common sense to at least guide you in the right direction.

While it is always important to remember that security professionals are human beings and are subject to making mistakes, it is also important to understand that people look for their security people to guide them in the right direction. So even if you are not sure exactly what needs to be done, you must be able to direct and lead people in the correct general direction.

For example, if there is a report of gunshots, that might not be covered in your employee manual but common sense would dictate moving people away from where the shots were fired and into a safe and secure location and out of harm's way. That decision would come from using common sense.

If there was a fire you would move people away from the fire in a safe manner telling them not to use elevators which could stop and trap them. Instead you would direct them to a stairwell far away from where the fire is. Again, this is just common sense.

Your common sense is pulled from past experiences and knowledge that you have learned over the years. It is the result of situations you have lived through. It is how you have seen things handled in the past and what the results of those situations had been.

Another reason that security professionals must have a good level of common sense is that the training and rules and procedures we are given are for the most common situations we will come up against.

Those rules and procedures cannot cover every possible situation or variation that may ever exist. There would be too many of them and the manual would be 3 foot think!

Instead, our training and our manuals give us the tools and knowledge to use when we find ourselves in a particular situation. We call upon that training and knowledge and then make a decision as to what is the best action to take. That is where our common sense kicks in. We look at the available options and figure out which ones are the best and then we take action.

Common sense might tell us the rule book is dead wrong at times. Sometimes we will have to make up the rules as we go along. When this happens, we need to use common sense and act in such a way that we can explain and defend our actions at a later time.

People are different and everyone reacts to things differently. There is no one "cookie cutter" approach that works every time. You need to determine what needs to be done and you must always use common sense when making those decisions.

Common sense lets you look at the situation and circumstances and factor everything together to determine the smartest and best way to move forward. Being able to act quickly and instinctively know the best approach to take will enable you to protect and safeguard everyone much better.

Physical Fitness

For some of you reading this chapter, you might read some things that make you uncomfortable and possibly angry or upset. But please understand that physical fitness is not just something to do with your appearance but also how well you do your job.

In previous chapters we had talked a lot about perception and when it comes to physical fitness, perception is very important. You must maintain a physical appearance that inspires confidence and safety. If you are 100 pounds overweight, that does not inspire confidence in your ability to move quickly, apprehend a suspect, or get yourself and others to safety quickly. Whether you can or can't, perception is everything.

Perception also plays an important role in discouraging people from breaking the law in the first place. If your appearance and persona tell someone that you are not someone they wish to deal with, that will make them tend to think twice about what they are thinking about doing.

Since the best way of protecting people is not to have them placed in danger in the first place, you want to discourage people in any way possible.

Think about body guards and security protection details. These assignments are usually given to well built and muscular guys who just look like they could take on anyone with little effort. They are big, they are intimidating and they have an effective presence about them. Rarely do you see a 5 foot tall 100 pound body guard or someone 5 foot 8 inches tall and 400 pounds. This does not mean that either of those people could not do the job, it's just that their appearance does not inspire safety and security.

The other important aspect of physical fitness is your ability to actually do your job. You need to be in good enough shape to run and climb multiple flights of stairs, pursue suspects, and react swiftly to any situation.

There will be times when an incident happens and you will need to run significant distances to respond to the problem. The longer you take to get there, the more potential danger people will be subjected to. If you do get there and you are exhausted and can't catch your breath, people will wonder about your ability to help them before you even get started.

Here are a few things to think about when it comes to physical fitness and your job:

Strength

It is important that you be physically able to handle basic tasks like carrying an average sized person to safety or carrying items like fire extinguishers and other tools of the trade up several flights of stairs as required. While you don't need to be able to bench press 400 pounds, you need to be able to handle routine tasks easily and safely.

Healthy

Security people should be in generally good health. Your health should not become an issue in how well you can do your job or your overall reliability. If you are not healthy enough to perform your job or keep regular attendance, then this presents a significant danger to others.

Just take care of your health and be aware of any issues or health related problems that might be interfering with your work and overall health. Get a physical once a year (or more often if your particular health requires it) to make sure you are taking care of your health.

Agility

Being able to perform certain tasks, often in less than optimum conditions, often requires a certain amount of agility. Often you will have to move through crowded areas or around obstacles and the ability to be agile and nimble is an asset.

This can because extremely valuable when chasing suspects or while running through crowded areas to respond to a situation.

Stamina

If you work in a large building or even a group of buildings like an industrial park or school campus, you will need to be able to get from one place to another quickly. You cannot rely on vehicles or elevators as they may not be available in an emergency.

Because of this you should have the stamina and ability to jog up several flights of stairs or run between buildings as needed. Just how much you will need to do will depend on the assignment and the building you are assigned to. No one expects you to be able to run up 100 flights of stairs on a skyscraper but you should be able to run up several flights as required.

It is also important to remember that once you get where you need to be you still have to have the energy to perform the tasks needed and be able to do those tasks at your best ability. This means that you cannot be out of breath and winded when those around you need your help or guidance.

Defense

Part of security is being able to defend yourself, and others, from the attacks of others. This does not mean you have to be a black belt in martial arts and be able to take out 15 people in 12 seconds.

But you should know how to defend yourself and be in sufficient physical condition to protect yourself and others when called upon to do so.

Most of the items discussed in this chapter can be improved upon or practiced. With a little effort you can increase your stamina and agility and increase your ability to lift and run. As far as weight is concerned and overall physical appearance, your doctor can help put you on a weight loss and conditioning program that will help with both.

Positive Image

When it comes security, image is everything. The image you project helps control the perception other have about you as a security professional. Many things make up your overall image and we have discussed most of them already. But since this is so important, let's discuss your overall image and what factors make up that image.

Appearance

It is often said that we only get one chance to make a great first impression. When it comes to your image, the first thing people encounter about you is the way you look. Though there is not one particular right or wrong way a security guard or professional must look like, we will only say that your appearance should be appropriate for where you are assigned and what tasks you are performing. Unless you are undercover in some capacity you should be dressed in an appropriate manner and you should be well groomed and clean.

There is no excuse for having dirty hands or a dirty face unless you were called upon to do something that got you dirty on the job. In those cases, wash up when you can.

Hair should be neatly trimmed and your face neatly shaven. No 3 day stubble or crazy facial hair! Shoes or other footwear should be cleaned and shined if appropriate.

Attitude

The way you act speaks volumes about how people feel about you. You can and should be confident but never cocky or arrogant. You should talk to people not down to them like you think you are better than they are.

You can empathize with people but remember that you are there to serve and protect within the rules and guidelines you are given.

Voice

Your voice is a very effective way to showing your emotions. Anger and sarcasm are readily heard in the way we speak. Your voice should always be calm and reassuring but forceful when needed. Always remember that you are there to make sure that people behave and act appropriately and that your directions and instructions are paid attention to.

Use your voice to calm people down and to communicate what needs to be done during a particular situation. But do so without being overbearing and dictatorial. You will have greater success with a more personal approach.

Conduct

The way we go about doing the things we do in life speaks volumes about the type of person we are and how we feel about others. If you do not pay attention to what is going on around you, or ignore people because you don't really care about them, people will notice.

If you violate rules yourself, how can you expect other people to follow your instructions? You need to set the proper example and follow all the rules. In fact, your conduct must be measurably better than anyone else because you are viewed as an authority figure.

You need to show respect to the people you are serving and protecting. That means not burying your face in a magazine or a book while at your desk. It means not making people wait because you are on a personal phone call. It also means being at your post so people can find you when they need you.

It is also very important to understand that both your conduct on and off the job will be taken into consideration when it comes to how people regard you. If you are neat and professional while on duty but are seen in the neighborhood sloppy and drunk at other times that will also factor in.

Like it or not how you conduct yourself at any time will matter when it comes to your image and the perception that people have of you. So take great care to always act and behave in a professional or responsible manner.

Past Acts or Experience

As people know you, their perception of you will be shaped by actual experiences instead of personal views and perception. They will see you perform on a daily basis and they will either become safer and secure in your abilities or become more skeptical if you do not do your job well.

It has been said that every negative experience can require as many as 10 positive experiences before the negative is forgotten. So if you do make a mistake, and we all do, just remember that you can overcome most mistakes and just do your best whenever possible.

Appropriate Values

When it comes to values and being a security professional, it is important to understand why your values help determine what kind of person you are and how effective you will be at your job.

The single most important value to have is the proper value of human life and what it means to others. You need to have a healthy respect for human life and what it means to other people as well. If you should happen to have little respect for life itself, then you will not give the appropriate care and effort to protecting it.

You also need to value and respect the rights, feelings, and wishes of others as well. People are different and therefore view things differently. You need to respect the needs and values of others and take them into consideration when dealing with people.

For example, religious values and beliefs often prohibit people from going certain places during certain times or eating certain food or performing certain acts.

You need to understand this and use this information when determining the best course of action. It is always better when we ask people to do things they are open to doing and not asking them to do things that are against their wishes or beliefs.

You should also be a person who respects the rules and regulations that are in place both within your organization and also within the people you are asked to protect or serve. Those rules and regulations have a purpose and we need to respect that and follow them. In other words, we need to set the proper example so others follow them as well.

Last, but definitely not least, we need to value people. We need to like and respect people and understand that each and every one of the people we are serving has a family that they are important to. We need to understand the need to keep them safe and out of harm's way. We need to understand the value of their possessions that we are entrusted to protect.

As a security professional, our main purpose and goal is to keep people, and sometimes their possessions, safe and secure. This is often not easy and sometimes tough decisions must be made. But with the proper values behind us influencing those decisions, we are far more likely to make the right decision and have the best possible outcome.

Part 2
Skills Needed

There are specific skills that a good security professional should have as well. In this part of the book we will take a look at some of the most important skills, why you need them, and how to get them if you do not currently have them.

Everything in this part of the book can be learned if you have the desire. It might take some time and it might take some practice, but these are important skills and well worth the effort.

At this point we should stress that these are only the most common and most important skills you will need. Depending on your own situation and assignment, you might need additional or different skills to enable you to do your job well.

Any time you have the opportunity to learn a new skill, or improve an existing one, you should take advantage of that opportunity.

The quality of our skills is what prepares us for success and growth in life. In other words, if you don't know it, learn it and if you already know it, improve it!

Experience

Experience can come in many forms. The most common and thought of types of experience is actually having lived through, or experienced something prior in life. When that happens, you are able to draw upon those memories to determine the best course of action.

Actually having lived through something is much better than reading about it or watching it on a video or even as a demonstration. While both of those options are still good for learning and building your skills, actually being part of a situation is still the best way to learn.

The longer you are a security guard or othersecurity professional; you will experience more different situations, more types and kinds of people, and become more adept at handling things faster and more accurately. Experience also enables you to react faster, and with more accuracy when you are placed in a certain situation.

Whenever we find ourselves having to do anything for the first time, we react more slowly and with uncertainty.

This is a normal reaction because we have never been called upon to do what is now required. So we take time to think and figure out what the right thing to do might be. All that thought and decision making takes time. Sometimes in tense situations, that time really isn't available to us.

But as we gain more experience, we find ourselves reacting faster and thinking less. Our actions and decision making process starts getting faster and more automatic. We react and do things more out of habit than from actual thought.

Another thing that happens with experience is that we make fewer mistakes or bad judgments. Everyone is human and we all will make mistakes but when we are new or inexperienced at something, we will make decisions based on limited experience and that makes a difference.

Experiences expose us to little things that might never be covered in our training. These things include how people might react, weather conditions, lighting, crowds, logistics, and other factors. These factors might have a significant impact on what we need to do and how we need to do it. We might make what we feel is the right decision only to find out by the results what we should have done differently. All of that information becomes available to us the next time we find ourselves in a similar situation.

The most common questions, or complaint, we hear is "How can I get experience if people require experience to hire me in the first place?" Fortunately, there are ways to get experience other than actual on the job experience. Some of them are:

Training Classes or Seminars

That is a very good question and this often creates a dilemma for people looking to start any job. Fortunately, though, you can get experience in other ways that will help you learn faster and better and make you a better performer.

We will shortly be talking about the importance of training and training is one of the best ways to gain experience in how to handle and behave in different situations or in learning a new skill set.

Training gives you an insight into something you are not familiar with. Whether it is learning something new or improving a current skill, attending a training session or seminar can be very helpful.

Think of a training session as getting the benefit of the experience of your teacher or lecturer. For example, if you are attending a seminar on crowd control, you would be listening to someone with experience on crowd control explain to you what needs to be done and why. They would likely use actual experiences and examples to demonstrate their actions.

These kind of sessions, where others use their own experiences to teach you, can be a very effective way of getting a real world education and gain the benefit of years of experience all within a few hours.

Hands on Training

Nothing beats actually doing something for learning purposes. By actually performing the task or skill, your entire body gets to experience what you are doing and you will be far more likely to remember what you were taught.

Just like you cannot get a black belt in martial arts by reading about the skills and maneuvers in a book, many other skills and techniques also need to be performed and experienced to do those best.

Observation

Sometimes just by watching something being done you can gain a great deal of knowledge in the process. When you stop and think about it, most of us do this many times over the course of our daily activities. We might go to a concert and really concentrate on what the drummer does because we play drums as well. Or listen to how the singer sings a particular song. We might watch a craftsman at a local crafts fair and learn how to use a certain tool. All the time the rest of the crowd just takes in the demonstration for entertainment purposes.

When it comes to security, we can watch other security professionals and see how they act and perform. Take note of what they do and how they do it. Now, keep in mind that it might be suspicious or downright creepy, for you to stand somewhere and watch someone. You might wind up being arrested or questioned! But you can learn a heck of a lot through observing others and start to develop your own skills in this manner.

Volunteer

Volunteering can be a great way of helping others out while at the same time getting valuable experience. Seek out possible volunteer opportunities in your area to see what you might do to pick up a little knowledge and experience while helping out your community at the same time!

Intern

Being an intern is sort of like a longer term volunteer position. An intern is basically an unpaid or low paid, person who works in exchange for experience in a particular area or industry. You gain some on the job experience while they get the benefit of you doing work for them at low or no cost. In addition, interning often is a good thing to have to place on your resume or work history.

Whatever you do to improve your awareness and skills will help you become not only a better security professional but also become better at whatever you do in life.

Experience gives us a different outlook on things. Experience lets us perform at a higher level and with better results and higher accuracy. Experience allows us to make fewer mistakes and become better at what we do and how we do it. So take advantage of opportunities as they become available to you. Observe what is going on around you and listen to those who have more experience than you do and learn from them.

Training

The proper training is important regardless of the occupation and security is no exception. In order to properly perform you must have the right skills and the right knowledge. The only way to obtain this knowledge is through proper and thorough training.

Training can be received through several different venues. From a structured college or university program to informal training seminars, training is within the grasp of anyone who wishes to get it.

Training gives us the knowledge and experience we need to behave and act properly in any given situation. Much of this knowledge is not available elsewhere so training is a vital part of our background. Training also exposes us to different methods of thinking and different ways to looking at situation in order to determine the best course of action.

Training is also not a one-time event or something that is only done at the beginning of our career.

Instead, everyone should be taking part in training classes each and every year to keep their existing skills current and to learn new skills and techniques as they become available.

For positions that require a certification, training is not only suggested but required in order to obtain, and keep, such a certification. In these cases, training topics will often be mandated but in any case should always be targeted directly towards the security industry and field.

Training helps give us knowledge and ideas to help us respond not only faster but more accurately and efficiently. By knowing the best way to act and respond in any given situation, we are more able to provide the highest level of security and safety for our customers.

It is strongly suggested that every security professional take at least one training class every year in our order to keep their skills current. While there are some very good training materials available on video as well, it is recommended that training be taken in a group so the student has the ability to interact and share thoughts and ideas with others during the training.

Training seminars are often available through local trade associations, law enforcement agencies and local schools and universities. Check with your local government or check with you manager or supervisor for known training resources and training requirements.

Observation & Comprehension

Security is an occupation that relies highly on the judgment and comprehension of the security professional. In order to provide the safety and security our customers and clients expect we need to be able to comprehend things that are going on around us.

While this might seem to be a pretty basic requirement, comprehension is more than just seeing what is happening around us. Seeing and comprehending are two different things. We can see things happening but understanding what those things are is something else entirely.

For example, some people can be in a room and not be aware at all of the things going on around them. They do not notice the people moving around or the activities taking place in the room. They are just in the room and that's about it. Whether they are waiting for someone or something or just there for a specific purpose, they are in the place but not aware of what is going on around them.

Naturally, that type of person would not make a very good security guard or professional. Someone in security needs to be aware of who is around and what is going on around them. After all, that is what security is all about.

Security is more than just reacting to something when it happens. It is even more about spotting problems and situations before they actually happen and minimizing or even eliminating the threat before it becomes a reality. This requires keen observation and comprehension.

First, though, let's talk a bit about the difference between observation and comprehension skills.

In their basic forms observation means seeing or noticing something and comprehension means understanding what you have seen or observed. It is very possible to observe something but not comprehend what you observed.

For example, you might be assigned to protect the people in a particular event and you might be able to observe everything going on at that event. You might see the individual people but not notice their actions or mannerisms that might make you alert to a possible problem. You might see 4 different people in the room but not notice that they are communicating with each other or are placed in certain spots which might make them a possible threat. While this might sound like a cheesy spy novel, this is where comprehension skills come into play.

In order to be an effective security professional, we need to develop our comprehension skills so that we can not only see the people in the room but also notice their behavior, appearance, mannerisms and other things that might give away their intentions.

For example, we might see a couple of individuals who might look completely normal in the appearance and behavior but we could observe a bulge in their jackets indicating a possible weapon or we might notice a look of nervousness or other outward sign that might alert us in some way.

A classic example would be to notice that someone came into a room with a briefcase or a backpack and then was noticed leaving without it. This is a minor feature but that person could have just left a bomb or other device in the room.

Criminals and people who are up to no good do not try and stick out in a crowd. In fact, they often go to great lengths to blend in and look the same as those around them. For example, if you are a guard at a childcare facility, someone looking to take a child might be dressed as a day care employee or as a young mother. You would not likely see an older man in a dark suit with a ski mask pulled over his face walk onto the playground! If you saw such a person, you would likely search them out and question them, right?

Security professionals need the skills to not only see what is going on around them, but also notice details and understand what they are seeing.

They need to be able to notice something that doesn't fit in with the surroundings. They need to notice behavior that is not appropriate or an appearance that does not fit in.

Much of these skills come from experience and training. They come from watching people and watching others at work. This knowledge also comes from listening to the stories and accounts of others who were involved in situations and what they saw and how they reacted.

Some people call it a "feeling" or a "6th sense" when they spot something that somehow doesn't fit or notice something that is wrong. But in fact it was neither of those things. It was that the person saw something that wasn't right and realized it. This is one of the most important skills any security professional can possess.

These skills can be developed by training and experience. Always be alert and always listen when someone is sharing their experiences with you. Read accounts of situations and new events to see what happened in those situations as well. Most criminals are not overly creative and will often do what others have done in the past. By becoming aware of those things we will be far more likely to spot those same actions and behavior in the future.

Fast Thinking

We have all heard the expression "thinking quickly on your feet". This means that an individual has the ability to think fast and make sound decisions very quickly. This is especially important when it comes to the field of security.

There will be times when a situation comes up where quick thinking will be required to get people to safety fast and get them out of harm's way. In some cases, lives may be at stake and time lost could mean lives lost. While it is not our intention to be overly dramatic, those situations do exist and you might very well find yourself in the middle of one someday.

People who are able to think fast are usually people with a lot of training and experience and are also fairly self confident. This combination gives them the knowledge they need to make the right decisions and the confidence in those decisions that makes it easy for them to act.

When we are not sure what to do we often hesitate and when we have very little confidence in ourselves we also hesitate. The result is that we often do not act as quickly as we should and people are place in harm's way.

For example, let's say we are in an area and we smell smoke. An experienced guard would know to get a few people together and start a process to move people out of the area to safety in a calm and orderly manner. The faster this is done the safer everyone will be. But if we should panic and yell out, or if we should delay starting the process, the fire might spread making evacuating people more difficult or even impossible.

Security professionals need to understand the rules, policies and procedures that are in place wherever they are assigned. They need to know who to contact in an emergency and they need to understand how they are to proceed during routine emergencies such as fire or during a robbery.

The more knowledge an individual has at their disposal, the more likely they will be to act quickly and proceed in the right direction. But acting quickly is very important in some situations.

If you are a person who has trouble making decisions or taking decisive action, that does not make you a bad person. But it might preclude you from being placed in a position of authority. If you are good at following direction then you will be a good person to have making sure people follow instructions they have been given. But you would not be a good choice to have as a leader or decision making person.

Again, the keys to thinking fast and making the right decisions are training and experience and knowledge.

The more training and experience you have, the more likely you will be to make the right decisions. The more knowledge you have of the rules regulations and procedures in place, the faster you will be able to direct people in the best ways to follow those rules and procedures.

Another critical part of thinking fast is the culture in which we work. If we work in an environment where people are supported when they make sound decisions, the more likely it will be that people make those decisions without much delay. But if people work in an environment where they are questioned and challenged, or even ridiculed for their actions that can change the way people respond.

We live in a very litigious world today where people are sued and brought to court for the smallest infraction. Thought that can sometimes be a strong factor in how we proceed or the judgments we make, we still must be aware that the safety and well being of the people need to remain our most powerful objective.

We need to make smart decisions, be able to back them up with solid reasoning and take the actions necessary to protect those who are placed in our care and protection. That means making sound choices and decisions quickly and acting upon them in a responsible manner.

Security professionals need to be able to be the people who are willing and capable of making tough decisions when they need to be made. We need take charge people willing to put themselves on the line when it comes to making those tough decisions.

Taking Initiative

Few things are more important than the safety and well being of the people and possession that we are entrusted to protect. Everything we do, and every decision we make, must be made with that security and well being in mind.

That means security professionals need to be people who are not afraid to take initiative and do what is required to make things go in the right direction. While we are not miracle workers, and while things will not always go according to plan, we must still be willing and able to take action when it needs to be taken.

Taking the initiative also means be able to see problems and faults in existing rules, processes, and procedures and bringing those to the attention of others so that they might e reevaluated and changed.

Things change over time and sometimes the rules and procedures do not change with them. For example, there might be a fire evacuation plan in place directing people in a certain direction for swift access from the building.

But that plan might have been done before a renovation and never updated. That route might not lead to the outside now and continuing to send people over that route might lead to serious danger. Alerting people to this would not only make things easier, but also lead to a higher degree of safety.

Taking the initiative also means sharing your thoughts and ideas when you see a better way to doing something that would result in a higher degree of safety for everyone involved. That might be a minor change in how something is done to the purchase of better or newer equipment.

Taking the initiative means always being aware and looking for ways to make things better and safer. It means looking for problems and discovering them before they actually become problems. Sometimes it might mean approaching something from the criminal's point of view and trying to find ways to beat security and then reporting those shortcomings to the proper individuals.

Regardless of what is involved, security professionals should always be on the lookout for any and all ways to provide a higher level of security for people, their possessions and other items of value that are entrusted to them.

Part 3
Conversation Skills

When it comes to providing safety and security to others, nothing is more important than the way we speak to and interact with others. Our conversation skills are the single most important tool, next to our eyes and ears that we can use to provide the highest level of safety and security to others.

It is important to remember that the accurate exchange of information between two or more people is the root of our ability to communicate. A single misunderstanding can place the lives and safety of others at risk. Because of this, it is important to understand what is involved with the communication process and how it affects the way we go about doing our jobs every day.

Most people understand that the words we use are very important when it comes to delivering our thoughts and information to others. But what most people do not often think about are two other factors that dramatically affect our ability to communicate efficiently.

Those two factors are listening and emotion. If we do not listen to the other people and really hear what they are saying to us, we might misinterpret the situation and make false assumptions. Plus, if we fail to understand the emotion behind the words, we might misunderstand everything and proceed in the wrong direction.

This section of the book will deal with several factors and how they pertain to our ability to communicate. It is crucial that we understand just how important it is for us to be able to communicate our thoughts and intentions accurately to others in all kinds of situations.

As security professionals, we are held to a higher standard and it is our responsibility to get the situation right in our minds. The responsibility to communicate clearly lies with us, not the customer or client. We need to be able to direct others in such a way that we get the accurate information we need to make the right determination and choice of action.

There are several things that every security professional must be able to do when he or she communicates with others. All of these are necessary to make sure the information exchanged is received accurately and that everyone has a full understanding of what has taken place and what need to happen next.

Good communication reduces chaos and stress as well as mistakes. It also reduces fear and instills confidence and reassurance. Good communication is the basis for everything that follows.

Be Good With Names

While it is not 100% necessary to know everyone's name, it goes a long way with people if you can refer to them by name and create an informal relationship with them.

Naturally this only pertains to people that you see many times over the course of a month or week. You cannot be expected to know, let alone remember, the name of every person who walks through the doors. But for building employees or everyday workers that come and go, being able to refer to them by name is appreciated.

Think about this for one moment. You just might be the first face someone comes in contact with when they walk through the door in the morning. You also could be the last face someone sees after leaving the office after a late night. So being able to greet someone by name with a friendly smile just might make someone's day go just a little better.

The other benefit to knowing and remembering an individual's name and being able to associate it with a face is that you are far more likely to recognize the person and be able to keep those individuals out of the building after they are terminated. Since some employees are known to become disgruntled and return to their previous place of employment intent on causing problems, you will be able to identify them and keep them away.

Another benefit of making someone aware that you know them by name is that you will discourage those individuals from stealing in the building. That is because in the back of that person's mind they are saying to themselves "Security knows my face and my name. I don't need that aggravation here!"

Being able to recognize and identify people makes it easier to find phone numbers and office numbers and to recover information faster when asked. It enables you to identify people faster in critical situations and be able to call someone by name to alert them in case of personal danger or other reason.

All of these reasons showcase the importance of being able to know and remember people's names. But perhaps the most common reason for calling people by their name is that it just makes things nicer and more personable. Much in the same way that doormen know the people living in their building, security people should know the people they are involved with as well.

Using names makes everything more pleasant, more personal, and helps the client or customer feel more valued. In turn this makes them feel more secure. And isn't that what security is all about?

Be Personable yet Professional

It is always preferable for security people to develop a professional relationship with their clients or customers. We just talked about the benefits of learning and using people's names in our dealing with people. That is just part of establishing a relationship with people.

We should start out this discussion with a kind of warning or disclaimer. The relationship between the security professional and his or her clients should LWAYS be a PROFESSIONAL relationship and never a personal one.

The reason for that is that there always need to be boundaries between the security professional and the client. If those boundaries are blurred or removed due to a friendship, that could place the client in danger or at least minimize your effectiveness.

A professional relationship allows you to interact with people using their names and learning their routines and other things while keeping your distances from their personal lives. This allows you to provide your services while still maintaining the professional / client relationship.

It is when the relationship turns personal where problems can start to turn up. People might think that rules or procedures no longer apply to them or that you will look the other way when they do things that they shouldn't. Clients or customers might not follow your orders or instructions because you no longer are considered to be someone in authority but rather a friend instead.

In addition, your judgment could be affected by a personal relationship to the point where you might not want to have something done, or demand that a rule be followed because of what the other person might think or feel. This can, and usually does, place both of you at potential risk.

During some kind of assignments, it might be hard to keep the relationship from turning into a personal one. This is especially true during protection details where people are together for long periods of time. Or when a person is assigned to a specific office or location for a long time. Over time boundaries can often get blurred and many times this happens without either party being aware that this is happening.

Keeping a professional relationship ensures that your instructions and commands will continue to be followed no matter what the circumstance might be. It helps keep the perceived level of authority in place as well.

It is very important that you realize that your success as a security professional rests on your ability to lead, instruct, and be followed. It does not rest on your ability to create personal friendships with those you are entrusted to protect.

Greeting People

It is important to be able to interact with those that you come in contact with every day. Being able to converse and smile and greet people is an important part of that interaction.

We cannot overemphasize the importance of a smile and a greeting when you see someone, especially first thing in the morning. You might be the first person that someone sees at the start of their day and a smile and cheerful hello will be appreciated.

A greeting and some interaction also makes you appear less threatening and more approachable. Or some people, the security uniform might be a little bit intimidating. We always want people to feel that we are there to help them and greeting them helps ease whatever tension or intimidation at might be present.

A personal greeting, where you refer to someone by name, is even more effective. When you do that, the person feels more important and appreciates the fact that you took the time and effort to remember their name.

As we have stated already, just the fact that people are aware that you know who they are might make them hesitate and think before they do something they shouldn't be doing.

When it comes to greetings, you should avoid becoming overly familiar. Do not use first names unless asked to by the individual you are talking to. You are safe with using "Mr." or "Ms." Or "Dr." Some people prefer this type of greeting while others might prefer first name greetings. As we said, use last names unless instructed otherwise.

It is also nice to wish someone a good night at the end of the day as well. It makes people feel good and that helps with how they feel about you as well. If you are aware of a special day like their birthday, wish them well on those days as well.

The best way to get yourself used to interacting with people is to make an effort just to acknowledge someone when you see them. If it is in the morning, say "good morning" followed by their name. Same for afternoon (substitute afternoon for morning!) and evening. For evening so can say something like "Have a pleasant evening" or something similar.

People like to be acknowledged and those people who shouldn't be there will shy away from your greeting or feel nervous and this might help you identify a possible threat as well.

Interacting with Different People

It is very important to understand that no two people are the same and no two people are going to react to everything in the same manner. While this usually does not create an issue or a problem in most situations, there can come a time when you might have to deal with this.

As we said, people are different from one another. Everyone is a product of all their experiences and influences from the time of their birth up to the current time. Everything they have experienced or been told up to that point will have influenced them in some way.

Part of these influences will also be culture and religion. These are important factors to consider because sometimes you might ask or require someone to do something that might go against one or more of their beliefs or customs.

That does not mean your instructions can or should be dismissed, only that there might be reluctance or problems caused by those instructions.

As we all know, sometimes there might be more than one way to accomplish something and alternative instructions might work better.

For example, some religions prohibit certain activities or actions after sundown on their Sabbath day. If you are aware of this and know that some of the people in your care share those beliefs, then you might make an effort to make sure certain things were completed before sundown. But you also need to understand that the safety of others is your prime concern. If someone refuses to take appropriate action and that decision places them, or others, in harm's way, you might have to take additional action.

Another problem that might surface with security personnel is dealing with people who have a problem with police or authority figures. These people might have had previous issues with Police or have negative interactions with them in the past. This is called emotional baggage and you will have to deal with it.

The best way to deal with all people is to treat each and every person with dignity and respect. That means being friendly and not yelling or ridiculing them in any way. It also means being respectful of their beliefs and values and treating them like you would treat your family and friends.

Another common barrier to communication and interaction is the language barrier. Not everyone speaks the same language.

Security professionals need to be able to communicate with most everyone so if there are a significant number of people who speak a different language, the security person assigned to that location should be able to speak that language as well as English.

Security people are usually called upon to resolve disputes and also to be a liaison between two or more people. Perhaps there is a question or disagreement and security is called to address it. Whatever the reason, you will have to place yourself into the situation and resolve it to the best of your abilities.

While we cannot get into great detail on this right now, let us just say that the best way to interact with people is to be as non confrontational as possible. Try to resolve the situation without blaming anyone unless the security breach was a serious one. Sometimes just reminding people of the rules or procedures is enough to resolve the situation.

Another way to resolve disputes and make everyone happy is to compromise. When arriving at a compromise, it is important to understand that this is not a winner and loser situation but rather you should try to make all parties winners. That means trying to give everyone as much of what they want or need as possible while still obeying and keeping within the rules.

Our primary concern always must be the safety of everyone in our building or within our responsibility.

Seeing that everyone is, and remains safe, sometimes requires a little creative thinking and finding alternative solutions. If we can do that while treating those around us with the dignity and respect they deserve, we will find our jobs and lives much easier!

Listening Skills

When we thinking about communication, we usually think about the word we speak and the emotions behind them. But there is another part to the communication process and a very strong case could be made that this part is the most important part of the communication process. The part of the communication process we are talking about is listening.

Listening is something we do really without thinking much about it. We say something, we listen to a reply or other comment and then we speak again. But we don't really concentrate or value the listening part and that is where the problems lie.

Really listening to what people are saying requires our attention and concentration. We must listen to everything others are saying and not tune them out when we think we have heard enough. That is a very common problem. We hear the first part of an answer, think we know the entire thought, and then interrupt or tune out the rest.

We also need to listen to and understand the emotions behind the words we hear. Something said in anger or frustration is likely not to be as accurate as something said in a calm and rational manner. In these cases, emotions can make us overstate something or even say something we truly do not mean. Surely you can recall instances in your life where you said something in anger that you later regretted. We all have.

When it comes to security professionals, listening takes on an entire new meaning. What we hear from others can have a significant impact on the safety and security of others. If someone is telling us something, we need to listen to everything that is being said and remember as many of the details as possible. If we fail to do that, we might forget something important that will either help resolve the situation or make something easier and faster.

For example, if someone rushes up to you to report that they saw a robbery in progress; you should wait to get the details. Where is the robbery? Who did they see? What did they look like? How many were there? And many more things. If you just rush off, you might find yourself in the middle of something serious without being aware of it.

Using the robbery example, let's say someone reported a bank robbery in progress. You get a few details like there were two men in the bank but you run off before the person could tell you that they saw two other men in a car out front and one of the street corners outside.

Without this knowledge, you might run in and get surprised by one of these other men. That "surprise" could come in the form of a bullet or other altercation.

Many people feel that time is important and they do not have the time to listen to someone ramble on and on about something. But the fact is, time spent getting all the information and all the details usually saves you more time than it takes to listen to them. Not only that, but the accuracy of what you do is directly proportional to the information you have when you make your decision. In other words, the more information you have, the better decisions you will make.

Now sometimes time is critical and there are people who love to take 20 minutes to give you 15 seconds worth of information. In these cases it is important to keep the person focused and ask them specific question in order to get the information you need to make the right decisions. When the person goes off on a side story, gently guide him back to the point and get the information you need.

If people appear excited or scared of afraid, get them calmed down first before you start asking questions or getting information. People who are frightened, excited or upset will tend to speak fast and not be as accurate as calm people are. We have mentioned that already and will do so again. Calm people are your best sources of quality information.

Sometimes you might ask yourself "how much information is enough"?

Well, there is no exact answer to that question because there are so many variables that could exist in any given situation. You might be under a time constraint if action has to be taken immediately to protect someone or you could have all the time you need. The situation could be very simple or extremely complex. Also, the matter could be a very minor one like a missing newspaper or a very important one, like an assault.

Generally speaking, the more questions you ask, the more complete your information is likely to be. The better and more accurate your questions are, the more detailed your information will be as well. But you can ask all the questions in the world and if you don't listen to the answers, you will miss out on potentially valuable information.

Here are some of the most common listening mistakes most people make:

Not Listening to the Complete Response – most people hear a response until they feel they have all the information they need. Then they jump to a conclusion before hearing all the information. This can lead to wrong decisions, wasted time, and wasted resources. In addition, allowing people to talk and continue their thoughts provides them with an opportunity to vent and calm down at the same time. This in itself is a valuable process.

Having Pre-Conceived Opinions or Attitudes – when people have pre-conceived feelings or opinions about someone or something, they tend not to listen to what someone is saying because they feel it is not trustworthy or accurate. Most of the time the opinion is about the individual speaking rather than the information itself.

Not Placing Value on the Source – if we feel the source of the information is not very good, we will not place a high value on that information and we will not concentrate as hard on listening to it. We are likely to become impatient or easily distracted.

Feeling Our Judgment or Thinking is Superior – most of us fall into this trap at one time or another. If we feel we have the answers, or we know more than anyone else, we will not likely listen to what others say unless they agree with us.

Contrary Information – many people tend to shut down their ears when they hear or are told something they don't like or disagree with. It is a well known fact that when most people hear negative words like "won't or can't" they shut down and never process anything that is said after those words are spoken. This is very common when dealing with customers or clients after you refuse a request. You might offer an alternative but they never remember that and will never mention that when they complain to others.

Interrupting Others – listening enable us to hear what the other person is saying both in the words and what is behind them. But there are a lot of people who continually interrupt others when they are speaking. This not only frustrates the other people but reduces the amount of information the listener takes away from the conversation.

While this is just an overview on the importance of developing listening skills, we cannot overemphasize the importance of learning how to listen effectively. The amount of information you will get from others by allowing them to talk and listening not only to the words but also the information behind them will help you immensely each and every day.

Accurate and complete information will allow you to act more accurately, respond faster, and perform at a higher level. It is well worth the time and practice in developing these important skills.

Remaining Calm

The ability to remain calm under a wide range of situations is more important in the security industry than in most other fields. That is because in security we are not only responsible for ourselves but for the safety and well being of others.

It is widely accepted that calm people make better decisions and remain more in control of their emotions and actions than agitated or angry people. Angry or frightened people are far more likely to act impulsively or without sufficient thought and those actions are dangerous not only to themselves but to others as well.

When it comes to protecting others as well as their possessions or personal property, remaining calm allows the security professional to make better decisions and to remain alert and aware of what is going on around them.

One of the elements that most criminals rely on is confusion and panic.

When people are in panic mode, they do not readily see what is going on around them. They do not notice people who shouldn't be there or activities going on around them that are suspicious in nature. This is the primary reason for inciting panic or creating diversions. All of those are intended to distract others from noticing what is going on around them.

Security professionals have another obligation and that is to help restore order and to keep the people around them calm and in control as well. It is difficult to keep others in control when you are in a panic! If you are a calming presence, you will promote calm in others as well. That leads to more orderly behavior and increased attention paid to details and instructions.

Most people say that while it is all well and good to say that you must remain calm, it is easy to panic when placed in a difficult situation. While we agree with that, there is an easy solution to remedy this from our day to day activities.

The most common reason people panic is fear and most of the time it is fear of the unknown. When people know what is going on and what they need to do, they are far more likely to remain calm. But when they have no idea what to do, if they have not been properly trained, then they get overwhelmed and they panic.

So the best way to avoid or minimize your panic is to increase your comfort level with the situations you come in contact with everyday.

Prepare yourself for possible situations in the future by making sure you understand what you should o in certain situations. Ask yourself what you should do in case of a fire, a robbery or other event and figure out what the best response should be in those situations. Learn all the rules and procedures that are already in place as those will help you as well. If something is not clear, or if you see a potential problem, discuss it with someone so you can make any changes that you think need to be made.

If we can have the training and knowledge to prepare us for problems before they become a reality, we will be more likely to face them in a calm manner.

Experience also helps us remain calm. After a while, as we experience different things, it takes more and more to get us nervous or frightened. This is not because the danger is any less, just that we had experienced it before and have developed a certain amount of confidence.

One word of caution however. Experience and training can lead to confidence and our ability to stay calm, but is should not lead to over confidence and risk taking. While we should be confident in our abilities and training we should never get to the point where we do not have respect for the situation and the danger it might represent.

Do not confuse respect for the situation with fear. If someone is looking to do you or someone else harm, you need to respect the threat and the potential danger.

It is all right to be afraid as long as it does not take hold of you and paralyze you or your judgment.

For example, if there is someone in an office with a gun, it is all right to be afraid of the possibility of getting shot. Fear gives us our notification that we need to proceed with caution. So in this case, that might mean calling for assistance or securing the area and waiting for others to handle the situation.

In that case fear tells us we should not rush in and confront the gunman. Doing so could result in harm to us and to others. Instead, fear tells us to be cautious and do think about what we should do and then do it.

But if our fear is so strong that it cause us to stop dead in our tracks and freeze, or run into a closet and hide, that is not a good thing.

Everyone experiences fear at several points in their lives. Fear in itself helps protect us from foolish actions. Self preservation is a strong drive in our brains. As long as we can control our fear and keep it in its proper place, we will do just fine.

But what do we do when we feel panic starting to come on? What do we do when we feel ourselves getting overwhelmed? If that should ever happen, it is important for every security professional to know and understand where to go to for help. Who to call for back-up, who responds to critical situations and who to call for what type of situation.

Being a security professional does not mean you are the sole person responsible for the safety and well being of others. While you might be the first line of defense, there are others that you can call to help you.

Never let yourself get to the point where you are overwhelmed or panicked. Reach out to someone else for help. That is the preferred course of action because it helps you protect yourself and others in the best way possible.

Tact and Reasoning

Sometimes dealing with people is not the easiest or straight forward task that it should be. People might be angry or upset for some reason or just have a problem with authority figures such as security personnel. Regardless of the reason, we still need to interact with these people and communicate with them in a productive manner. This is crucial to our success as a security professional.

First of all, let's make no mistake about one thing right from the start. How people treat you is no reason to treat people in the same manner. If someone is rude to you, that is not an excuse to be rude in return. The people we are entrusted to protect or guard are our customers and we need to always treat them with dignity and respect.

Most of the time there are more than one solution to our problems. It is up to us to figure out the best way to respond to a problem.

If our problem concerns an individual or group of people, we need to figure out a way to resolve it tactfully without overly embarrassing or shaming people.

If you can resolve or avoid a problem without assessing blame or having a confrontation, then that is probably the best way to react. For example, if someone violates a parking rule and it doesn't cause a problem, it might be best to tell the person that there is a rule against parking there and also give a short explanation as to the reason. Sometimes that is all that is needed to keep that person from doing it again and everyone is happy. But if you yell at him in front of people or condemn their actions harshly, then that person is likely to respond in an aggressive manner to you. The result is an ugly confrontation over something minor that winds up causing everyone major headaches. If they do it again, however, then proceed with a stronger response.

Rules and procedures will govern you through most of these situations but there is almost always a certain amount of discretion that can be used on your part to give a better result.

Another important thing to remember is that if someone does violate a rule or does something they shouldn't have done, talk to them about it privately. Do not chastise them in front of other people. This might embarrass them and they might feel the need to act strong in front of others and you will find the situation escalating for no reason.

Do any kind of discipline privately unless the matter is serious and you need a witness.

The best place for this would be in the security office or someplace quiet. The security office is good because it is "your turf" and you would have some amount of emotional edge in discussions held there.

People do not react well to being cornered or forced into admitting guilt. While sometimes this is necessary, there are times when just allowing someone a graceful way out is the best approach. Using the parking example, you could start off by saying, "We've been noticing people parking there and it is causing a problem. You really aren't allowed to park there so we would appreciate it if you would refrain from doing so in the future.

What you have done there is make the person aware that they have done something wrong while at the same time given them a "way out" by telling them that others have done the same thing. This approach is far less threatening but still gives you the opportunity to make sure they are aware of their mistake.

Now there may come a time when someone does something that just cannot be let go without some kind of punishment. An assault or something where damage was incurred has to be addressed in a firm manner. But in these cases, you must still deal with the person with dignity and respect no matter what their attitude towards you might be.

When it comes to soliciting information from people, you also need to use some tact and not accuse people or make them feel guilty for some reason.

You can ask generic questions designed to draw out information without assessing blame or suspicion. Remember at this point you are just trying to get information, not solve a problem.

It is important to remember that how you interact with people is going to affect the way they perceive you and your ability to do your job. If you are too lax in enforcing the rules, people will break them with increased frequency. But if you are too harsh or accusatory, that information will spread quickly and their attitude towards you will not be positive.

To take this one stop further, it is important to understand that your conduct must be above reproach in all dealing with clients, customers and even strangers. If you treat someone poorly, or if you are rude and disrespectful, you might find yourself up on charges or at the end of a lawsuit for violating someone rights. While such suits might be baseless, your conduct will be brought into question and can be used to impeach your credibility. That can cause problems with other legitimate things that you had done in that situation.

If there is a way of resolving a situation calmly and without confrontation, that is usually the best road to take. Talk to people in a calm and respectful manner and use tact when it comes to your questions or statements. This will enable you to get more co-operation and information from people and make your overall job easier and more productive.

Be Easy to Understand

All right, here is one of those subjects that might tend to annoy you or even make you angry. In some cases, what we discuss here might not be viewed as politically correct. But being understood is extremely important when it comes to security and we must make every attempt to insure that the words we use and how we use them, allow us to be understood by others.

There are a few issues that cause us to not be understood by others. Here are a few of the most common:

Language – If we cannot speak or understand the language others are using, then we cannot expect others to understand us. Depending on your assignment and area where you work, you might be called upon to speak more than one language. If that is the case, then you should be chosen because you already have that ability. This is required if there is a known significant population of certain language speaking people in the area in which you are working.

If that is the case in your assignment, speak to your supervisor and make them aware of this. When more than one language must be spoken, it is good practice to repeat each instruction or command in each common language.

We Talk Too Fast – The speed at which we talk is very important when it comes to getting our message and point across. Some people talk so fast that it is difficult, or downright impossible to understand what they are saying. This is especially true when you are talking to someone over the telephone and all you have to go by are the sounds that you here. Rapid speech stops being about words and starts to become gibberish. If this is a problem with you, make a conscious effort to slow down the speed at which you talk. Do not make it so slow people think you are making fun of them and think they are stupid, however. Just slow it down a little so people can understand.

We Talk with a Heavy Accent – Some people talk in a very heavy accent and that makes it difficult to understand especially if there are unfamiliar terms or information being discussed. Simple words might be able to be understood but complicated word, or technical information can be especially frustrating. If you have an accent, please understand that people may have a hard time understanding you. Try to speak slower and more clearly. Perhaps a speech class might be a good idea if you find this problem happening often.

There is no shame in this; it is just a perception and understanding problem that just needs to be addressed.

We Mumble or Talk too Low – We all know people who talk very low or even appear to mumble instead of talk. We need to speak at a level sufficient to be heard by normal hearing people and also be heard above any background noise in the area. If people have to strain to hear you, they will likely miss some of what you are saying or misinterpret something they thought you said because they couldn't hear it well enough.

We Use Long or Too Technical Words – This is a problem in almost any industry where there is industry terminology or jargon used. People use huge and unfamiliar words when they should be using shorter and more readily understood words in their sentences. It's like a car mechanic telling you that he had to "interchange the electric ignition initialization anti theft interface" when he should just say "I replaced your ignition switch." Some people are not aware what your industry jargon might be and others do not understand long and complicated sounding words. Your goal here is not to impress others with your vocabulary but to get result and be understood. So the next time you are in a situation do not say "Incendiary condition exists please promptly vacate the immediate location" just say "FIRE! Please exit the building now!"

We Don't Establish Eye Contact – When you talk to people, try and look at them. Do not stare but make sure you are facing them so they can see your lips move. Most people cannot lip read very well but the combination of seeing the lips move while hearing the words spoken will result in a higher level of comprehension. In addition, should there be someone who is deaf or hard of hearing, being able to see your lips as you talk will help them understand more as well.

We have said this before and it bears repeating. The responsibility of you being heard lays with you not the other people. As the security professional, YOU are the one who needs to be able to direct people and tell them what they need to do. If you cannot do this in such a way that the vast majority of people understand what you are saying, that may place others in danger or in harm's way.

So use easy to understand words; talk at a speed which enables most people to understand while not being too slow.

Effective Body Language

Much of what we communicate comes from the way we look when we say it. Depending on the situation sometimes more than half of our communication comes from things other than words. The other parts come from how we stand, the expression on our faces and other physical clues that we send out to others.

There are studies after studies that go into great detail about the subject of body language. You can agree or disagree with parts of these studies but one thing is 100% dead on accurate: Body language plays a huge role in the way we communicate.

With that in mind, let's discuss some of the ways body language plays a role in the life of a security professional.

Some of us are very good at controlling our emotions. We can act calm while we are close to panic inside and we can hold our voice steady when we are frightened to our limits. But controlling words and speech is much different from controlling our posture and our expressions.

Think about what people communicate over the phone. They hear words and they hear the way those words are spoken. They can hear fear or anger and they can feel sarcasm and disinterest. But if we are careful, we can minimize those signs by careful speech and a few deep breaths.

But if we were having the same conversation in person, you might see someone who is angry talking with their arms crossed which is considered a defiant or contentious position. They might see you sweating and realize you are afraid or nervous. They might watch you wring your hands constantly or pace around and be nervous. All of these things are visual indicators that give people insight into the way you are feeling at that moment.

As a security professional it is important that you exhibit signs of strength and confidence. People rely on you to protect and lead them and they will not feel secure if you are sweating or acting nervous or scared.

Body language can be minimized by careful observation and awareness. If you become aware of a habit you have when you are nervous, you can work on that to eliminate it. You might even determine that therapy might be needed to control those types of behavior. But the first step is awareness. Once you become aware of something, you acknowledge that it exists and you can take steps to resolve it. But if you remain unaware, nothing will change.

Personal space is another important consideration that you need to be aware of.

Around everyone exists a space that we call our own personal space. As long as people remain outside this space, we are comfortable. But if someone gets too close, or leans in and violates that space, we become nervous and defensive.

So make it a point to keep a fair distance away from people you are talking to or questioning. Unless physical closeness is required to help or protect someone, keep your distance. If someone starts to show signs of nervousness, then move further away if possible.

Never crowd or lean into someone while talking. This is viewed as extremely aggressive and the situation can quickly deteriorate. Keep your distance and keep other calmer by keeping yourself calm.

Raising your voice is also seen as threatening by most people and people often get defensive and start raising their voice. Since little gets accomplished when everyone is yelling, try and keep your voice down unless you need to alert or warn someone.

Other gestures people do not respond positively to are rolling of the eyes, which signifies you don't believe someone, shaking of the head and sighing which might indicate frustration and outwards signs of hostility or aggression. These items should be eliminated or at least kept to a minimum.

In another area, there are things we do that help give people the wrong impression of how we might be doing our job.

If we sit behind the desk and read magazines all day and not acknowledge anyone, this gives the impression that you don't care or are not aware of your surroundings. Neither of these is a good thing to think about someone in the security business.

If you ignore people waiting to speak to you in order to carry on a personal conversation that indicates that you feel your conversation is more important than theirs. That is not good either. People should always be made to feel that they are your number one priority.

But enough of the negative things. Let's talk about some positive things you can do as well:

Keep Eye Contact With People While Speaking – always look at people when you are talking to them. This adds a personal touch to the conversation and makes people more relaxed and comfortable. Your eye contact makes people feel more valuable and appreciated.

Always Have a Smile on Your Face, Never a Frown – A smile can make someone feel good and can disarm someone who is angry or looking for trouble. Always remember we are looking for things to do that reassure people and make them calm. Nothing works better than an honest smile. Don't overdo it, just be natural. On the reverse side a frown can make you appear unapproachable and this will be viewed as a negative by most people.

Extend Your Hand for a Handshake When Applicable – Anything you can do to make your interaction more personal is a good thing. An offer of a handshake when appropriate is often a good thing.

Focus on the People, Not a Magazine or Your Television – Make sure your clients and customers feel that they are you first priority. Leave the magazine and portable televisions home and concentrate on your customers. During really slow or overnight shifts reading might be allowed but it should never interfere with interacting with people. Music players and headphones should not be used because not only do they distract you, the headphones will interfere with your ability to hear outside sounds. This may make you unaware of trouble or calls for help.

Be Warm & Friendly Not Cold or Withdrawn – Security professionals should always be polite and friendly while at the same time keeping the relationship professional. You want to appear friendly but professional so that people respect and acknowledge your skills but are not afraid to approach or interact with you. It is a delicate but critical balance.

Be Helpful When You Can – People like other people who offer help and assistance when needed. Make sure you are ready to help when needed and try to offer before being asked. This will enhance people's perception of you.

Speak in a Calm and Soothing Voice – No one likes to be yelled at or talked down to so make sure you speak in an easy to understand and calm voice. Your voice should be pleasing to the ear.

The visual aspects of communication and not readily understood by most people but are still very important when it comes to interacting people and making the correct impression. We urge you to be aware of how you stand, your mannerisms and the way you talk. Ask family members and co-workers if there is anything you do that needs to be worked on or addressed. It could be very much worth the time and the effort to correct a few little things that could have a major impact.

Confrontation Management

Unfortunately, part of the security professional's duties often involve resolving situations and handling confrontation. This can be a very difficult and challenging process and how we go about it might mean the difference between success and failure.

There will be three basic types of confrontation you will be called upon to deal with. The first is confronting someone who has done something wrong, broken a rule, or violated a rule or law. The second is dealing with an altercation between two or more people that is starting to escalate. The third, and most critical is the confrontation that involves immediate danger or threatening of life.

Confronting someone who has broken a law or violated a rule is the easiest and we should always attempt to resolve those situations without harsh behavior and with either a warning or a fine if warranted.

Most people understand this type of confrontation and though there might be a dispute in what actually occurred, there is usually not much of a problem.

In these situations it is important to gather the correct information as well as proof should the other person question or dispute your claims. The information can be in the form of reports, statements from witnesses and photos that clearly show the violation. Follow existing procedures for filing complaints and always be fair and respectful.

The second kind of confrontation, where you are called upon to resolve or break up a confrontation can be more difficult and time consuming. The first call you need to make is whether the confrontation or situation is within your control or whether you need to request assistance or back up.

For example, two people arguing about a fender bender in the parking garage should be able to be handled without assistance. But if you are called to respond to a situation and you find 50 people fighting or weapons involved, it is best to call for assistance and back up. Always remind yourself that you cannot adequately protect anyone if you yourself are injured or rendered helpless. Your personal safety is also a valid concern.

Resolving any confrontation requires negotiation skills and the ability to break down the situation into manageable parts. The first step should be to get all parties to calm down.

This might be as simple as asking them to calm down or you might have to separate the people in order to talk to each one individually. But always remember the first thing to do is get people to calm down.

Once you get everyone to calm down, find out what the issue or problem is and see if it is something you can resolve. If you can, fine, just go ahead. But if it involves something you cannot control, then you need to figure out whom else needs to get involved or where you should direct the people involved.

For example, let's say something happened in a store that angered 30 customers and started a riot. You would get people calmed down, find out what caused the situation and determine who needs to get involved to resolve it. In this example you would need to get the store manager, or even area manager involved. You would provide a report of the situation to all parties and inform everyone of whom they should contact. If the authorities are brought into the matter you should follow established procedures for interfacing with them to provide assistance, information, and direction.

Lastly, you might have to respond to situations where there is a perceived or actual threat to human life or injury. Naturally these are the most important and significant situations and will require the utmost care and special handling.

When you are confronted with such a situation, you first thoughts should be about how you can get as many people into a safe situation as possible.

This would include directing people towards safety, restricting access to the area, and other duties.

For example, if you were informed of a hostage situation or an armed robbery in progress, you would want to stop people from entering that area. You would secure the area and keep people from entering a potentially dangerous location. If a fire was present, you would help people to a safe area while keeping people from entering the area where the fire is located. In most cases multiple people would be required to cover all access points and help evacuate people. Get assistance and back up as required.

Part of the process is also assessing the situation. While someone might report the issue, or you might respond to an electric alarm of some kind, you will need to have someone confirm the problem exists and provide an estimate of the situations severity. It might be a false alarm or it could be a real fire, burglary, or security event. In any case, follow established procedures and let people know what you are responding to and what you need done. In other words, coordinate everyone's efforts so no resources are wasted or duplicated.

After the situation is evaluated and as many people are moved to safety as possible, it is time to try and resolve the situation. In most cases, this will involve the local authorities and they will take charge of the situation. In other cases, however, depending on the type of security services you provide, it might be you or your co-workers handling the entire situation.

When that occurs, be sure to follow established procedures including proper notification of others and follow standard negotiation and response procedures. Always act with the safety of as many people as possible in mind.

When it comes to your personal security, we often have to walk a fine line. While your personal security is important, as a security professional you are expected to remain on site and direct people to safety and act on their behalf when it comes to making sure everyone is safe and secure.

This does not mean that you have to rush into a burning building to search every room to make sure everyone made it out alive. But it also means that if you are notified that there is a fire that you just can't yell "FIRE!" and then run right out the door! As we said, there is a delicate balance between your personal safety and the safety of those in your care.

Every situation is different and there are legal issues in place as well. So we suggest that you follow existing and established rules and procedures as closely as possible. Do whatever you can to help as many people as you can. Be there to supply directions, provide instruction and support as many as you can for as long as you can.

Like a lot of other things in life, no two situations are going to be exactly the same. Use your best judgment, get as much training as you can get and always use common sense when following rules and procedures.

Your ability to communicate clearly and accurately and keep people calm will serve you well in handling and resolving most conflicts. Use common sense in your conversations and do your best to help everyone involved. Your goal is to keep everyone safe and secure and that should always be your main objective.

Empathy

Before we close out this book, we wanted to talk again about the importance of empathy. Showing empathy does not mean admitting guilt or telling anyone that they are right or wrong. All it does is let someone know you feel for them in their current situation.

It is sad but today with the way things are we must be very careful in what we say and do. Or we could have those words or actions held against us in a court of law. But that does not mean we have to stop being caring human beings.

It is all right to comfort someone who has become injured. We just should do that without stating that someone was or was not at fault. We can let someone know we understand when something has happened without sharing sensitive or inflammatory information.

In other words, do not stop being a responsible and caring human being. Just take a moment to think about what you want to say and make sure you chose your words and statements carefully.

This goes not only for actual conversations both in person and over the telephone but for any printed information as well. This would include, but not be limited to, e-mails, letters, reports, online postings of any kind or any other digitally recorded media such as voice mail.

Legal Issues and Considerations

In this book we talk a lot about following procedures, rules, instructions, protocols and other guidelines. All of these things are well and good and they are all intended to help you perform your duties in an organized and structured manner.

But you also need to understand that those rules and other things must not differ from the Federal, Local and State laws that govern them. If any rule or procedure calls for you to do something that is against any law, you should bring that to the attention of everyone involved. That would be your manager, supervisor, or boss. They should see that those issues and problems are quickly addressed.

We are not lawyers or have legal training when it comes to responsibility under the law. But you should not willingly violate any rule or ordinance or law at any time unless there is no other choice.

You should always respond within the law and make sure you have your actions and conduct covered before you act.

We strongly suggest you address any legal issue and concerns with your attorney and with your company if you have any questions or concerns.

Conclusion

The materials covered in this publication should give you a pretty thorough idea of what it takes to prepare yourself to become a world class Security Professional.

These skills and attributes have been clearly shown to be valuable tools to help every Security Professional perform at their best and provide the highest level of protection and security to those in their care.

But having these skills and attributes is only part of the equation. In order to perform at your best you need to use these skills and practice and refine them. You need to constantly look for ways to improve your skills and master them.

In other words, you need to practice these skills until they become habits. Until you perform them without thinking. Perfecting them and doing them until they become second nature and you can call upon them within seconds. When you reach that point you will find yourself respond faster, more accurate and providing a level of service that every Security Professional would be proud of.

Even then you are not done. Just like a doctor must keep up to date on the latest treatments and an auto mechanic has to be trained on the latest systems, the security professional must always look to find the best new skills and the latest information so that their skills remain current and effective. Everything changes in this world and we must change along with it or find ourselves left behind.

Though you might not think so, providing security services to others is a very important and worthwhile process. People entrust you with their possessions and their lives. It is an awesome responsibility but a very rewarding one as well.

Do not take this responsibility lightly. Always do your best, always act with the safety and security of other as you utmost priority, and always treat people with dignity and respect.

Do that and everything else falls in line.

For more information about Customer Service and Customer Service Training, please go to our website at:

http://www.infowhse.com

Be sure to sign up for our newsletter and get a FREE Customer Service E-Book!

Printed in Great Britain
by Amazon